BAD TURNED GOOD
A SECOND CHANCE

DR. JOSEPH JENNINGS

Cover by: Risen Underground
& Erika Leal

© Copyright 2012- Dr. Joseph Jennings

Published by: **Not By Chance Publishing-2012**

NCP

Not by Chance Publishing

P.O. Box 3561
Ft. Pierce, FL 34948-3561

ISBN 978-0-9838928-1-6

All rights reserved. This book is protected by the copyright laws of the United States of America. It may not be copied or printed for commercial gain or profit. The use of quotations or occasional page copying for personal & group study will be granted only upon request.

For more information please contact:

**Dr. Joseph Jennings
Second Chances Outreach Ministries, Inc.**
P.O. Box 549 Tyrone, GA 30290
Ph: 770-599-1629
contact@josephjennings.com

Years ago I met a couple who in time, would become my dear friends. When my wife asked me if there was anyone I would like to acknowledge or dedicate the rewrite of this book to, without hesitation I answered Gerald & Mary Jo Boman!

Thank you both for standing with us in the high times, but more importantly never leaving our side in the low times. As Ecclesiastes 4:9-10 says, "Two people are better off than one, for they can help each other succeed. If one person falls, the other can reach out and help. But someone who falls alone is in real trouble." I really believe there is so much more God desires to do for the kingdom through our relationship!

Dedication

I dedicate this book to my loving wife, Lindsay Fulton Jennings.

Special Thanks

Dr.'s Fred & Betty Price
Crenshaw Christian Center- Los Angeles, CA

Dr.'s Mike & Dee Dee Freeman
Spirit of Faith Christian- Temple Hills, MD

Pastor Dayne & Lisa Massey
Grace Point Church- Peachtree City, GA

Fred & Teresa Foote
Heritage Mark Foundation- Lansing, MI

Gerald & Mary Jo Bowman
Stuart, FL

This book is a much needed tool to a lost & hurting generation of kids: Kids who don't know any way out of the darkness, kids who have not grown –up with the advantages of being raised in a Christian home or with Christian Parents, kids who have been labeled bad because they had no other choice but to grow-up in bad environments without knowing any other way. These kids are simply good, but they are lost & hurting and they need to know there's another way—this way is God's Way! He is the way, truth, and life. This book is a tool to teach them in their new life; a life which only Jesus can give. To the kids who are about to read this book: I don't know you, but I LOVE YOU with a mother love; and I pray for you to be all that Jesus wants you to be. Keep walking toward the light.

Leah Trescone
Just a Mom

Dear Friend,

Very seldom have I met a family more precious than Dennis & Leah Trescone. Whenever I walk through a fiery furnace, and I need a supernatural covering of prayer, I call Leah. Some people just know how to get through to God with a right now attitude. Over the years, I have not mastered the art of raising money, but I have been blessed with prayer warriors from all over the world. Leah Trescone is one of those.

Dr. Joseph Jennings

Table of Contents

1. Do Gangsta's Go To Heaven?
2. Leave Da Kids Alone
3. A Second Chance
4. Does God Remember All Of The Bad Things I Used To Do?
5. Beginning Again, Again
6. I Am Brand New
7. The Bible
8. Praying Soldiers
9. Da New Family
10. Wow! They Might Hate Me
11. Holy Spirit & Fire
12. Prisoner Of The American Dream
13. Remember Your Assignment
14. "Bad Boy Turned Good" Pictures

1
Do Gangsta's Go To Heaven?

In the summer of 2006, I found myself in a familiar place, taking part in FICWFM, a large Christian convention, in Los Angeles, California. Normally, I would only be speaking to the teenagers at this particular event, but somehow I ended up preaching at both a youth session as well as being one of the keynote speakers for several thousand adults.

I was amazed at first, and almost overwhelmed, by the invitation to speak to the adults. What an awesome door God had opened.

Then came the big question. What message could I possibly relay to this group of pastors and church leaders? In attendance would be some of the greatest pastors and teachers in the country, some with mega churches and anointed, gifted T.V. ministries.

I prayed and sought God as to my message and in the process, I quietly laughed to myself. "What in the world would I be able to preach to them?" Most of them could teach Holy Ghost circles around me. But I had learned three rules early on in ministry: Don't be moved by the size of a church, by who is in attendance while I'm preaching, or by the amount of the offering.

Then God spoke to my spirit, telling me to simply remind them of their "Assignment".

I preached that day simply from Mark 16:15-16, "Go ye into all the world and preach the gospel to every creature. He who believes and is baptized will be saved, but he who does not believe will be condemned."

I reminded them that our assignment with God was, is, and always will be about souls. Thank God for prosperity, healing, and big churches, but the end result should always be souls. The Bible says that the greatest miracle ever performed is not the growing of a leg or the raising of the dead, but bringing a soul into the kingdom of God. Proverbs 11:30 reads, "And he who wins souls is wise."

I shared with the group, my frustration of being a front line foot soldier and sometimes attacking enemy territory with no cover. For years, most of our financial support came from secular people. I would have to think that the priority of any church and/or Christian, their bottom line, would be winning souls. But so often, that's not the case. Right or wrong, I'm not going to judge. Like a good soldier, I got my orders. A wise preacher once told me, "Stay in your lane Joseph."

That's exactly where I'm at, in my lane. I fly low and slow, but I'm in my lane. Sometimes I get spiritual road rage and even get a little crazy, but God has graced me well.

One of the greatest outpourings of the Holy Spirit involving our ministry came while participating in a networking of ministries through the John Guest Evangelical Association in Birmingham, Alabama.

I was the featured youth speaker for assemblies at the local junior high and high schools. There was basically an uproar after some anti-Christians in the community found out that I was not only a motivational speaker, but an Evangelist as well. To make matters worse for those people, the next day, I was on the front page of the second section of the newspaper advertising the citywide outreach.

That article was a blessing in disguise. Because of it, we had a supernatural turnout. Thousands of youth and gang members from all over the city attended.

I gave my testimony that night and talked about my 14-year drug addiction, my violent, dysfunctional family, and my years as a gang leader. I explained to them that the choices they make would come with a price. The price I paid is evident.

I have thirteen bullet holes in my body and three bullets still inside me to this day.

Toward the end of my presentation, I felt a stirring in the crowd. Before I could even finish, kids starting walking down the aisles. 2,500 people responded to the alter call, hundreds of them being gang members. Some cried, while others were caught up in the excitement of something never experienced before. This was a modern day move of the Holy Spirit.

Because of the various gangs represented, my street senses were overloaded, telling me, "Watch out!" Something was wrong. Something was out of place.

Satan always comes to kill, steal, and destroy and at that moment, I felt his evil presence.

As I glimpsed to my left, there he was in the midst of it all, operating through a notorious Birmingham street gang. In the middle of the alter call, they had a formed a circle around a young female gang member, raising her up in rank right there. It blew my mind. I was already on guard, as I knew there were multiple gangs at the alter and the whole outreach could have been destroyed.

But we serve a greater God.

Isaiah 59:19 says, "When the enemy shall come in like a flood, the spirit of the Lord will lift up a standard against him and put him to flight."

In Matthew 16:18, Jesus tells Peter, "I will build my church and the gates of hell shall not prevail against it."

A young ex-gang member from the area, by the street name of "God's Gansta" nudged my arm, as we had seen the same thing at the same time. We jumped off the stage, screamed and headed for the circle. They started to disperse immediately, knowing they'd been caught and now, street challenged.

We had the juice. It was our party. And our righteous God was the only true gangsta in da house!

I blew up at those who were still standing around as to the falsehood of their gang doctrine. I was angry that they had the audacity to try to pull this crap off in the middle of what God was trying to do. It was one thing to disrespect the meeting, but totally different to disrespect the Holy Spirit.

In Acts 5:1, Ananias and Sapphira did the same thing. They lied to the Holy Spirit and died behind it.

Those kids had no idea the amount of disrespect they had just shown. It was such a spiritual and physical drain on me. Yet, we went right on worshipping God and praying salvation to the rest of those at the alter.

That night, I tossed and turned, falling into such a deep, violent sleep, that I broke the flesh of my lip by biting it. I wept and had nightmares the rest of the night. I woke up the next morning with my pillowcase covered in blood and tears, still having a very clear vision of my dream. It dawned on me how, in the process of trying to help the gang members, I might have signed their death warrant.

My mind raced to the word of God, to Matthew 12:43-45 where Jesus says, "When an unclean spirit goes out of a man, he goes through dry places, seeking rest, and finds none. Then he says, 'I will return to my house from which I came.' And when he comes, he finds it empty, swept, and put in order. Then he goes and takes with him seven other spirits more wicked than himself, and they enter and dwell there; and the last state of that man is worse than the first. So shall it also be with this wicked generation."

Although there were so many saved that night, where would they go now? Who would want them? What church would let them in on Sunday morning looking the way they looked? They were only kids with baggy pants, funny hair, and some with bad attitudes. They would bring no great tithes and offerings. Many of them didn't even know the depth of their decision. They were just kids looking for a new family and a way out of hell.

By this time, I was feeling so alienated, and rejected, remembering all the negative voices from so-called Christians over the years telling me reaching out to the lost was all a waste of time. If there's no one to do the follow up, where do all these converts go?

For months after that night, I was angry and confused as to the call of God on my life. Was I out of the will of God? Was I really wasting my time?

Then God spoke to my heart.

Remember your assignment Joseph.

2
Leave Da Kids Alone

Everything starts and ends with the word of God. It isn't about man's interpretation, or being politically correct, but above all else, what does God say?

You'll find it in John 10 verse 27-29, which reads, "My sheep listen to my voice; I know them, and they follow me. I give them eternal life, and they shall never perish; no one can snatch them out of my hand. My Father, who has given them to me, is greater than all; no one can snatch them out of my Father's hand."

Now that settles it for me.

I once heard a tape of another youth preacher talking about a time in his life when he was bombarded with a lot of summer speaking engagements.

After participating in a couple of outreaches, he was boarding a plane, physically exhausted and complaining to anyone who had ears. A flight attendant, noticing his solemn face, asked, "Is everything all right?" He simply repeated what he had been saying to others. "I have all these meetings to do," he complained.

After finding a seat on the plane, and stowing his luggage, he tried to calm himself. He said the Holy

Spirit began to speak to him saying, "You don't HAVE to do anything. You GET to do it."

For me, that was not only a ministry lesson, but a life lesson.

I GET to minister to youth. I don't have to, but I get to. And I feel honored God has called me to this assignment. I have a mandate on my life to rescue lost souls. There are thousands of preachers lined up, that would love to have my anointing and my assignment. But like a good soldier, my arm is continually raised and I'll be like Isaiah who said, "Here I am. Send me." Send me anywhere to anyone at any time.

As I carry out my assignment, reaching kids around the world, I find so many that have low self-esteem, broken families, and no value. Often times I tell the girls that they draw boys who they think they deserve. And the truth is most of them don't feel like they deserve anything. Thus they end up with a jobless, loser who doesn't even love his own mother, let alone have a relationship with God.

I tell them again and again that they do have value, but their value is based on their choices… not past mistakes, not gang culture, not clothes or money, but choices. Life is about choices, destiny, purpose, and finding out who you really are.

If I can get just one point across, I want you to see and understand just how valuable God thinks you are.

You ARE valuable. Now all you have to do is believe it!

God says in Matthew 18:1-4, "At that time, the disciples came to Jesus and asked, 'Who is the greatest in the kingdom of heaven?' He called a little child and had him stand among them and he said, 'I tell you the truth, unless you change and become like little children, you will never enter the kingdom of heaven. Therefore, whoever humbles himself like this child, is the greatest in the kingdom of heaven."

The bible tells us that the way into the kingdom of heaven is by the simple trust and dependence of a child. And the way to greatness is by the humility of a child expressed in humble service.

Sometimes the older we get, the harder it is for us to hear the voice of God. We need to pray that adults would be open to child-like faith, ushering in a modern day move of God.

Evangelist Billy Graham has said for years that the majority of those who accept Jesus Christ as their Savior, are 19 years old and younger.

You would think that a major priority of the church and ministries would be more geared toward youth, if in fact winning souls is wise.

Matthew 18:5-6 says, "And whoever welcomes a little child like this in my name, welcomes me. But if anyone causes one of these little ones who believe in me to sin, it would be better for him to have a large millstone hung around his neck and to be drowned in the depths of the sea."

God doesn't like ugly. Leave his babies alone.

Can you imagine a millstone hanging around your neck, weighing one thousand pounds, as you are thrown into the sea? Dang! What a trip.

Matthew 18 verse 10 reads, "See that you do not look down on one of these little ones for I tell you that their angels in heaven always see the face of my Father in heaven."

Simply put, we are not to think less of childlike believers because they are honored in heaven. The word of God says their angels are likely guardian angels of the highest rank.

No matter what your age, or when you accepted Christ, you'll always have guardian angels watching over you. Remember you ARE valuable and this book was written just for you.

3
A Second Chance

I never really believed in longevity or second chances. I always lived for today. Tomorrow was never promised and I knew any day I could die over nothing. But then one day, I was truly given a second chance.

I actually believe that I was given more than just one second chance, but multiple chances to start over throughout my life. One incident that I remember in particular, I was in Memorial Hospital in South Bend, Indiana back in my wild days. I had been admitted to the emergency room with multiple gunshot wounds. All I can remember hearing were people screaming that I was going to die.

As a heathen, I was again reminded of the angel of death and his presence filled the emergency room. He had come for me. As I was being wheeled into the operating room I heard one last shout," Jennings is going to die!" I desperately grabbed for the hand of who I thought was a nurse and said," They're going to kill me!" To this day, I remember her face as she smiled and said, "No, they're not."

I survived the operation that day. Many years later, as I was holding court on a local street corner, I was confronted by a woman who said, "You don't know who I am, do you?" I replied, "No." She went on to tell me she was the lady from the operating room. She gave me her name, and by the time I had turned around, she was gone. She had disappeared.

I believe over the years, I have had numerous visits from angels. Most of the times, I never heeded their messages. Like a lot of you reading this book, you've had a hundred second chances. Now it's time to serve God.

Choosing to become a follower of Jesus Christ is the most important decision you will ever make - a decision that has eternal consequences. Congratulations! You are now a soldier in the army of the Lord.

Would it surprise you to learn that God, as your Creator, has been anticipating this day since the moment you were conceived in your mama's belly? One writer in the Bible exclaimed, "You have known me from my mother's womb." Another wrote, "How precious it is, Lord, to realize that you are thinking about me constantly!" Sounds incredible, but the God who made you also watches over you. That means you really matter to God.

The Bible says that the God who made the universe has always had YOU on his mind. It claims that, as the Creator, he has always had a longing in his heart to have a relationship with those he has created.

Think about it. What if these claims are true? How would they affect the way you live? Thinking about these ideas will leave you with a sense of excitement. Almighty God thinks about me? He really cares? Millions have experienced radical change in their lives by embracing these thoughts. God will have that affect on you.

Jesus taught his followers, "The truth will set you free." Your decision to journey through life as a committed God soldier has set you up for new levels of freedom and changes.

The Ultimate Party

According to the Bible, a party began when you first accepted Jesus. Jesus said in Luke 15:10, "I tell you, there is joy in the presence of the angels of God over one sinner who repents." That was you in living color!

Before we talk about the partying that is going on, let me explain the terms used by Jesus in this verse. In the Bible, a sinner is not necessarily a horrible, hateful person. A sinner is a person who has chosen NOT to journey through life trusting God. To repent simply means to do a "180." Instead of walking away from God, you turn around and start walking toward God, building an inner trust in him.

Another verse from the Bible also reveals that some partying is busting loose in heaven: "He will rejoice over you with shouts of joy." God really does celebrate over what you have done and even writes your name in the book of life!

Why? Because God is big on family and he's got your back!

One of the early Christian writers wrote, "God's unchanging plan has always been to adopt us into his own family by sending Jesus Christ to die for us. And he did this because he wanted to."

No gang, homie, boyfriend, girlfriend, or anyone else has ever paid that price for you!

Turning to God is only possible through the work that Jesus did on the cross. When you receive Jesus Christ as Lord (to call him Lord means you surrender control to him), it brings you into a family relationship with God, the ultimate family that many people spend a lifetime trying to achieve.

As a follower of Jesus, you have become a child of Almighty God, the Creator. That is what deciding to follow Jesus has accomplished. It's the thing that makes God celebrate!

A Child of Satan

You probably did not realize it, but before you opened your heart to Jesus, you were in a "family" relationship with the enemy of God, Satan. Jesus spoke directly to the people who were not God-followers in John 8:44. He said, "You are of your father, the devil."

That did not mean they were walking around like lifeless zombies with dark circles around their eyes. It just meant they were out from under God's influence and under Satan's. They were children of the devil.

So often thugs, gang members and dope dealers are controlled sub-consciously by Satan to destroy and hold hostage their own neighborhoods. They have become the 21st century Ku Klux Klan.

Many people don't want to hear it, but the devil, or Satan, is not just some cartoon-like hood rat with a pitchfork, horns, and a freaky tail. He was once a great angel who served God. This angel, named Lucifer, later decided to stop serving God and actually tried to overthrow him by attacking God's throne. With one command, God threw him to the earth in total defeat. If anybody is a righteous gangsta, it's God!

Since then, this fallen angel, the devil, has tried to come against God by coming against the object of God's love – us! Satan tricked the first man, Adam, into betraying God. This betrayal paved the way for Satan to control the whole human race. I'm talking about all of us. Ephesians 2:1-2 says:

"Once you were under God's curse, doomed forever for your sins. You went along with the crowd and were just like all the others, full of sin, obeying Satan, the mighty prince of power of the air, who is at work right now in the hearts of those who are against the Lord. All of us used to be just as they are, our lives

23

expressing the evil within us, doing every wicked things that our passions or our evil thoughts might lead us into."

You all know what I'm talking about! Many of you took part in the drugging, clubbing, even the gang banging and often times didn't even care.

But get this. Only those who open their lives to Jesus and his work at the cross experience deliverance from Satan and experience the freedom of becoming sons and daughters of God. Now that's what I call cool!

I once preached a radical message, while on tour with Ron Luce's "Acquire the Fire" outreach, titled "Born to Raze Hell!" It literally caused an uproar when teens found out they were born again to raze hell! The bible explains in 1 John 3:8, "The reason the Son of God appeared was to destroy the devil's work."

Ephesians 6:1 says, "Be imitators of God." If we are to become imitators of God, we have been instructed to do what Jesus did – destroy (raze) all the institutions of hell. We have orders from above to raze hell!

Aren't you glad you made the choice to roll with Jesus? He is now your Savior, your daddy, your doctor, your psychologist, your homie, and everything else you'll ever need. He has saved you from all that you were as a child of Satan. You are now God's child. Satan has no more right to control your life. Jesus Christ is on your side to help you follow God. That being said, be prepared for the greatest challenge of your life! Although there will be good times and mountain top experiences, there will also be valleys and storms. But storms come and storms go. No storm lasts forever. Just remember Jesus is Lord, even over the storms of life.

First Corinthians 10:12 and 13 says, "So if you think you are standing firm, be careful that you don't fall! No temptation has overtaken you except such as is common to man; but God is faithful, who will not let you be tempted beyond what you can bear. But when you are tempted he will also provide a way out so that you can stand up under it."

You made the right choice when you decided to become a soldier for God. Opening your life to Jesus sets you on the path of freedom and victory. He is more than Almighty God, and the Creator to you. He is your Father. And that is good news.

You have some demanding days ahead as you get to know your new Father through prayer and through what he says about himself in the Bible. Get on it!

Questions:

At the end of each chapter from here on out, we have provided questions about the information you have just read to help you apply what you've learned. Don't cheat! Study. I'm watching you.

1. What do you believe it means to be a child of God?

2. Read what Romans 8:12-17 and verses 27-39 says about being a child of God. Summarize these verses in your own words.

3. Think about the phrase "child of God". Write a list of words that come to mind when considering this phrase.

4. Think about the phrase "child of Satan". Make a list of words that you believe describe life as a "child of Satan".

5. Look at your lists from questions #3 and #4, then write a sentence or two that expresses why being a child of God is far better than being a child of Satan.

6. Why do you think making a commitment to be a follower of Jesus Christ is the most important one you will ever make?

4
Does God Remember All Of The Bad Things I Used To Do?

People talk about thugs who sell drugs, but until you walk in their shoes, you'll never understand. Malcolm X once said, "I'm not going to sit at the dinner table and everybody is eating but me. If you don't give me something to eat, then I'll take it."

That's what my life was all about: selling drugs and stealing just to survive.

The dope game was just a way of life. I sold drugs on all different levels. One day my bag was weed, then cocaine, then heroine. Anything that could be sold, I'd sling.

One day I'd dropped off a big bag at my people's place and I'd come back to check my money. While at the dope house, I was caught off guard by one of my homie's mom. She had pulled me into a large closet. She had found out the dope was mine. With tears in her eyes, she pleaded for one fix to get her through the day. She fell to her knees and offered to do anything I wanted her to do.

I almost lost my mind. How in the world anyone knew it was my bag was beyond me. I threw her the dope and ran from the house. That was too much power for me.

Sometimes I would sit and wonder… "Will I be judged for this one day?"

Does God remember all the bad things I used to do?

God owed us death because of our connection with sin! Romans 6:23 says, "The wages of sin is death."

However, God figured out a way to free us from our death sentence. Jesus Christ came to earth to take our blame and to cancel the effect of sin upon our lives. John 1:29 says, "John saw Jesus coming toward him and said, 'Look, the Lamb of God, who takes away the sins of the world!'"

Jesus willingly came and took the death we should have gotten for our rebellion (sin) against God. The whole "cross" deal was done for us. Jesus Christ suffered and died for you and me. He experienced what we should have experienced. His blood was spilled instead of ours and now that blood is said to satisfy justice (which demanded we each die for our sins) and it "purify us" from our sin. 1 John says, "The blood of Jesus, his son, purifies us from every sin."

The way that God thinks, every one of the stupid, evil things you did in the past can now be forgotten. You are forgiven. That means there is no reason for you to live under the guilt of what you have done in the past. No matter how bad you have blown it, God has made a way to cleanse you and make it as though it never happened. Your friends and family may remember, but God won't and he will help you get past the judgments of people. God's forgiveness is stronger than all the terrible things you have done.

I heard it best explained by Pastor Dayne Massey of Gracepoint Church. He said, "Righteousness is the ability to stand in the presence of God without guilt, shame or feeling insignificant, as if sin has never existed." There's nothing you can ever do or say to make you more righteous in God's eyes than you already are right now. No matter what you've done in your past, the good news is that what God does will always outweigh what we do. All we have to do is trust him.

Romans 5:20 says of us, "But where sin increased, grace (God's favor to forgive) increased all the more." Many have committed unspeakable crimes like murder, rape, incest, etc. and feel that God could never forgive them. But this verse from Romans 5:20 declares that God's kindness and forgiveness will override anyone's sin! That includes you!

In Bible days, the word "forgiveness" was used in reference to the releasing of a prisoner. It literally means "to send off, to release, to let go or let be." But my favorite definition is "to hurl away like a missile."

When you trust that Jesus died for you (in your place), and that his blood was shed for you, it causes all your sins and failures to be hurled from you like a missile blasting away. They leave forever!

What a picture that paints for us. When God forgives us, he blasts away our sins. There is no evidence in Heaven that they were ever committed by us! Now that's phat and delicious!

"As far as the east is from the west, so far has he removed our transgressions from us."

"For you have cast all my sins behind your back."

"He will again have compassion for us; He will tread our iniquities underfoot. Yes, Thou wilt cast all our sins into the depths of the sea."

These verses claim we don't have to live in the guilt of the past. What if these verses are true?

Romans 3:23-24 says, "Yes, all have sinned; all fall short of God's glorious ideal, yet God declares us 'not guilty' of offending him if we trust in Jesus Christ, who in his kindness freely takes away our sins."

Though there are times we need to make amends for the wrong we have done by trying to repair the damage we have caused others, we don't have to walk around condemned or feeling like we can never make it in life because of all our wrongdoing. Romans 8:1 says,

"There is therefore now no condemnation for those who are in Christ Jesus."

God never remembers your past; the bad news is that Satan never forgets it. Satan, the enemy of your spiritual life and your trust in God, would love to continue controlling your life through guilt over the past. By doing so, he can keep you locked into old habits and destroy your future by replaying the memories of your past. But your past cannot be used against you now. The Bible claims you are a child of God. You don't have to identify with your past life; you have a new life in Christ. What does that mean? We'll talk about that next.

Questions:

1. The Bible tells us in Romans 6:23 that the "…wages of sin is death." How is it possible that God does not have to give us what we deserve (death)?

2. In your own words, define "forgiveness". According to the Bible, how does God feel about your past sins?

3. Why is it so difficult to "feel" forgiven even though we know by God's words that we are?

4. What important lesson does this teach us about out "feelings"?

5. Has anyone ever hurt you, wronged you, or mistreated you? How difficult was it (or is it) for you to forgive that person?

6. Do you think God can help you forgive those who have hurt you? Won't you stop and pray for God's help now?

5
Beginning Again, Again

A few years after I'd been saved, I was in a local gas station in Palm Bay, Florida. I had just finished touring with "Acquire the Fire" and leading hundreds of kids to the Lord.

It was a relaxed day. I was wearing shorts and flip flops, pumping gas and heading for the beach.

A monster truck pulled into the gas station with a redneck driver at the wheel. As soon as he noticed me, he stopped his truck, leaned his head out the window and shouted, "Who are ya?" I knew he wasn't talking to me, so I paid him no attention. Then he shouted again, directly at me, "Who are ya?" By then, I had jumped straight into my flesh and the gorilla inside me woke up. All I could think of was all the times I was harassed by white racist fools. "What?" I yelled. All I could think about was pulling that pump out of the gas tank, spraying him down, and setting him on fire. The gorilla was awake!

All of a sudden, the Holy Spirit slapped me across my head and said, "Fool, you're still under the anointing." You see, people's spirits are drawn to God's anointing, and not to man. I missed an opportunity to witness the gospel of Jesus Christ. I later apologized and repented in a sermon about acting stupid. There will be times when you too, will miss God or act foolish. What can I say? My spirit is willing but my flesh still gets weak sometimes.

Thank God for forgiveness and for allowing us to begin again, again.

God did a miracle inside you when you opened your heart and started your journey of faith. The Bible says your very nature, your essence, changed. 2 Corinthians 5:17 states, "Therefore, if anyone is in Christ, he is a new creation; the old has gone, the new has come!"

What does that mean: you are a "new creation"? It means there is a part of your being that has been transformed or made new. Let me explain. The Bible describes people as being three basic parts; spirit, soul, and body.

Just like an astronaut needs a space suit to live in space, we need an "earth suit" to live here. The body is our earth suit.

The soul is the part of us that thinks, reasons, and makes decisions. It also is the part of us that expresses emotion.

The spirit is the part where your conscience exists- the part of you that knows right from wrong. Your relationship with God is a spiritual thing. It starts within your spiritual part, your spirit. Jesus said, " God is spirit, and his worshipers must worship in spirit and in truth." When most people relate how faith dawned in them, they refer to the fact that they just knew inside that they needed to open their lives to Christ. Responding to that knowing and opening your heart to Christ is what causes you to become a "new creation". Neither your soul part nor your body part becomes a new creation - the miracle occurs within your spirit.

When your spirit is re-created, you become God's child. Sinful behavior and wrong influences can no longer rightfully control you!

Concerning this, God said, "I will give you a new heart and put a new spirit in you; I will remove from you your heart of stone and give you a heart of flesh. And I will put my Spirit in you and move you to follow my decrees and be careful to keep my laws."

This miracle has happened inside you – that was the difference you felt when you asked Jesus to become a part of your life. God took out the old you (spirit) and put in a new you. You are a different person inside than you used to be. You are a new creation!

This miracle is so deep that sometimes it doesn't dramatically touch your emotions. Many don't feel that much different coming to Christ but have new inner longings and priorities. Don't be concerned about that. The greatness of this miracle is not determined by how much feeling you have.

You may not feel anything spectacular or out of the ordinary, but you will notice a difference in your life. For instance, before coming to Christ you may have felt a little guilty about saying or doing bad things. Now, you are going to discover a much stronger reaction in your heart. You will find yourself being very sensitive to the wrong that you do – you will hate it. The reason is you now have a very new nature. The old part of you that was devoted to sin has been replaced. It is as though you have been born…again. Are you with me homie?

And that is exactly what has happened as you came to Jesus and entered the kingdom, or influence of God. Jesus said in John 3:3, "I tell you the truth, no one can see the kingdom of God unless he is born again."

Now you won't feel comfortable getting angry with people or talking ugly about them. You won't feel good about destroying your body with drugs or alcohol. You won't let yourself follow the passions and lusts that you knew before coming to Christ. Sex with someone you are not married to has to stop. Now you're a gangsta for God!

This won't happen because you decided to become a goodie-goodie, but because God's nature of purity has been deposited into your new re-created human spirit. "No one who is born of God will continue to sin, because God's seed remains in him; he cannot go on sinning, because he has been born of God."

This does not mean you will never slip back into the old ways to which you were accustomed. It means that when you do, you will not feel comfortable with it – you will long to make such things right again. Before coming to Christ, it was never such a big deal to sin. Your reasoning went something like, "After all, I am only human."

That reasoning won't work anymore because you are no longer just human- now you are a child of God. You are different and you know it. Because of his presence in your life, you will sense his displeasure whenever you fall back into sin and you will want to distance yourself from the sin instead of from him.

Repeats

If you find yourself slipping back into old patterns of sin, in a repeat of the past, just call upon Jesus again. He promised to help us when we are tempted to return to wrong patterns of living.

"Because Jesus himself suffered when He was tempted, He is able to help those who are being tempted."

When Jesus physically left this planet, He did not intend to leave us struggling on our own. He said in John 14:18, "I will not leave you as orphans; I will come to you."

If you get tricked, or played, and find yourself back in sin, run to Jesus. He will cleanse you again and again when you fail. 1 john 1:19 says, "If we confess our sins, he is faithful and just and will forgive us our sins and purify us from all unrighteousness."

Jesus is faithful to forgive us no matter how often we fail Him through sin.

Knowing this will keep your faith strong through failure while you are still learning how to live in a new way. (We'll talk about that next.) It takes time to learn how to break off Satan's influence in your life, so don't get discouraged.

You don't have to be perfect. God just wants you to grow.

Questions:

1. Explain the "new creation."

2. Why would the change in our souls (mind, will, and emotions) not be instantaneous?

3. Trusting our feelings to accurately determine our spiritual condition is unwise. Explain why.

4. List your behaviors and character traits that you would like to see God change.

5. Why can we still be hopeful after we fail or lapse into an old sinful behavior?

6. According to 1 John 1:9, if we slip back into sin, how often will Jesus forgive us? At what point in time does He forgive?

7. What should you do if you start feeling hopeless about being able to change?

6
I Am Brand New

Once I preached at Crenshaw Christian Center in Los Angeles, California. Earlier that day I had made a visit to East LA to meet with various crip gang members. One of them was Gregory Batman Davis, one of the original ten, who co-founded the crips in 1969-70.

I had invited him and some of his boys to come to the church that night just to hang out. I never thought in a thousand years that after I'd preached and given my testimony, he would respond to the alter call and receive Jesus Christ as his Lord and Savior. He walked down the aisle with his shoulders back and head up just like a true soldier.

Later on, we would debate as I challenged him to understand the word of God that says in 2nd Corinthians 5:17, "Therefore, if anyone is in Christ he is new."

He kept spouting gang talk: Once a crip, always a crip. For hours we went back and forth. Finally we came to the conclusion that our spirit man is saved and born again, but yet we still maintain an understanding and love for the hood and our people.

Being a gangsta is simply a mentality, a way of order.

There are good gangs and bad gangs just like there are good preachers and bad preachers.
There are good republicans and bad republicans, good democrats and bad democrats. It's how they protect and represent the people that matters.

The bottom line is bringing life and hope to a dark world.

Jesus said, "I have come that they may have life, and have it to the full."

Jesus came to bring us a brand new way to live. As we saw earlier in Ephesians 2:1-2, "Once you were under God's curse, doomed forever for you sins. You went along with the crowd and were just like all the others, full of sin, obeying Satan, the mighty prince of power of the air, who is at work right now in the hearts of those who are against the Lord. All of us used to be just as they are, our lives expressing the evil within us, doing every wicked thing that our passions or our evil thoughts might lead us into."

But now, because of what God has done within our hearts (making us new spiritually), we have a brand new kind of life within us. Paul claims, "You are living a brand new kind of life that is continually learning more and more of what is right, and trying constantly to be more and more like Christ who created this new life within you."
What does he mean when he says we have a "new life?"

Before coming to Christ, you were in control of your own life. In other words, you had a certain way that you had learned to live. How you made your choices, the kinds of entertainment in which you participated, the way you spent your money, how you reacted to pressure and confrontation, how you managed your sexuality, how you treated others, the music you listened to, etc. all formed your lifestyle.

Just as a tea bag spreads throughout all the steaming water in a tea pot, so sin spreads throughout your whole being; spirit, soul, and body. Sin is the nature of Satan. In other words, your whole life was controlled by Satan's staining influence. Your choices (i.e. entertainment, music, spending habits, relationships, etc.) were all influenced by the power of sin.

When you came to Christ, your spirit was cleansed from the "tea stain" of sin. Now the Holy Spirit can influence your choices and actions. According to 2 Peter 1:4 we can "participate in the divine nature and escape the corruption in the world caused by evil desires."

As we learn how to let that "divine nature" (or the nature of God) win our minds and bodies, we will see a new life of wholeness and holiness emerge!
We don't have to continue living the way Ephesians 2 describes by allowing the devil to force us to go "along with the crowd". We don't have to go on "obeying Satan". We no longer have to live our lives "expressing

evil" and "doing every wicked thing that our passions or our evil thoughts might lead us into."

Now we got it goin' on and God can be in charge!

Because of this, the way you make your choices, the kind of music you listen to, how you spend your time and money, the way you react to peer pressure and confrontation, your work ethic, who you hang with, etc. must be re-learned as a soldier in God's army.

It's important that you understand that this "new life" is present only within your spirit. You still have to wash up, brush your teeth, and put on deodorant! The challenge of your faith will be to learn how to tap into the unseen things God has done in you in order to change your choices and actions on the outside.

This can be difficult to learn and practice, but you've got to hang in there. The habits of your former life are often hard to break, especially if you still have the same "dirty" friends.

Can you imagine a homie from the streets becoming an astronaut? How about their reaction when he or she reached zero gravity for the first time? Simple things like eating, moving objects, going to the bathroom, etc. would be a real challenge. What was "natural" for them on the earth doesn't work anymore because the rules have changed. They would have to concentrate on and re-learn how to do the simple things they used to do without much effort while on the earth.

Yo! The same is true for you. You are now in a whole new place. You'll have to concentrate in order to grow in your new life in Christ. When pressure or problems or opportunities come, you can't respond the way you used to respond. You'll need to pause and concentrate in this new "zero gravity" life and practice going against what was "natural" to you. The rules have changed homie! Get up on it!

The Flesh

Though you have been made a "new creation" inside (in your spirit part), you still have your soul and body to deal with. The soul and body are influenced when we trust in Christ, but they haven't totally changed yet (and won't completely until we get to heaven). The unchanged, "tea-stained" parts of our soul and body form what the Bible calls "the flesh." The flesh is the part of you that will want to continue doing wrong even though you are now a follower of Jesus.

The flesh is also called the "sinful nature." It's kind of a weird, Dr. Jekyll / Mr. Hyde thing: one part of you resists and hates sin (the new, clean nature in your spirit), but you also have a part of you that will push to keep practicing the sins you used to do before you came to Christ (the flesh).

Think about it. Until you get to heaven, there will be part of you that wants to do right and a part that wants to continue doing and being wrong. That means you can expect a bit of a war to be going on inside you for some time.

That is exactly what happens inside every believer. The nature of the flesh, or the sinful nature, fights with the God-like nature of your spirit (where the Holy Spirit lives). Paul talks about the battle that takes place as these two natures fight to control your life.

"So, I say, live by the Spirit, and you will not gratify the desires of the sinful nature. For the sinful nature desires what is contrary to the Spirit, and the Spirit what is contrary to the sinful nature. They are in conflict with each other, so that you do not do what you want."

If you want your spiritual nature to win in this battle (instead of your flesh) you must learn to identify with your spiritual part. Let me explain.

For instance, if you have strong desires to do something that you know is wrong, like drinking a forty, smoking' some weed, or bumpin' up in some club ("Drop it like it's hot!"…You know what I'm talking about!), don't think, "Oh no! I want to do wrong again. I wish that I wouldn't want wrong things anymore!

You've basically said, "I am flesh - a sinful person. I'm a failure." That kind of thinking gives sin power in your life. All you've really done is come face-to-face with the flesh and found out you're not perfect.

What you need to do is identify with your new nature and scream, "Yo! Wait a minute! This is wrong. I don't have to continue following my old sinful urges! God has made me a new person; a new creation. Jesus, you are connected with me now. I trust in you. I don't have to follow the urges of my flesh part (which is inspired by Satan). Satan cannot control me anymore! Jesus, please help me get my focus right. I am being tempted to do something that is wrong!"

Here you identified with your spirit nature. You have said, in essence, "I am a spirit-a spiritual being, a new person, a person connected to God and saved from a life dominated by sin and Satan."

By identifying with your spiritual nature you win the battle between the spirit and flesh. Though this war will not end until we go to heaven, we can win every time we enter into battle IF we learn to call on God in the middle of it!

Watch out! Don't play games with your flesh. Any time you sense it wanting to do wrong, pull out your spiritual AKA assault rifle and bust a cap in that attitude or desire. Don't pass go. Don't collect $200. Don't even reach for that cell phone to call a friend. Whenever you start feeling tempted, run to God. Tell him what you are feeling. Thank him for what he has already done in you and ask him to help you do what is right. You will discover that God doesn't expect you to act right in your own strength. He just wants you to come to him and he will drown out the wrong urges and thoughts.

Romans 6:19 says, "In the past you offered the parts of your body to be slaves to sin and evil. You lived only for evil. In the same way now you must give yourself to be slaves of goodness. Then you will live only for God."

As long as you <u>keep running to</u> and presenting yourself to God, you will not be controlled by sinful impulses. If you stumble and let those impulses take over again, don't panic. God is bigger than sin. You aren't, but God is. <u>Run back to him</u>. Decide that no matter how often you fail you will never give up and simply surrender to a pattern of sin. Satan will try to get you into a mindset that is impregnated with hopelessness. He wants you to believe you can never change - so you might as well give up. <u>Don't give in to that lie.</u>

If you refuse to submit to the impulses of your flesh and decide to turn to God for help, you will destroy (or crucify) the power of the flesh to control your life.

Just like Jesus was crucified on a cross, we must "crucify" (or put to death) our sinful nature (flesh) by refusing to be controlled by it. "Those who belong to Christ Jesus have crucified the sinful nature with its passions and desires."

It may take awhile for you to figure out how to consistently run to God to preempt sinful actions. If you will stick in there, you will smile as you see God break the power of bad habits in your life! Being free is a good thing.

All you have to do is keep going back to God and asking him to forgive you. The wonderful thing is: God is more faithful to forgive you than you are faithful to sin. 1 John 1:9 says, "But if we confess our sins, he will forgive our sins. We can trust God. He does what is right. He will make us clean from all the wrongs we have done."

Now that's the bomb.

Water Baptism

When the first Christians came to Christ, the very first thing they did was to get water baptized (or immersed under the water). It was a step of obedience to God for them. It was also a symbol they could think about again and again to help them identify with their new life in Jesus. Let me explain.

In baptism a believer is placed under the water. This symbolizes our being placed in the grave with Jesus. God isn't trying to be freaky. He is trying to get us locked into the idea that everything that Jesus did was done for us. Water baptism symbolizes that.

Jesus came to earth to take away our sin. At the cross, he took upon himself the very thing that made us evil - the sinful nature, or the flesh.

The Bible says, "For God took the sinless Christ and poured into him our sins." The last part of this verse tells us why, "Then, in exchange, he poured God's goodness into us!"

There was a divine exchange made on the cross when Jesus died. He exchanged his holy nature for our sinful nature. He was placed in the grave after this exchange. Three days later he came back to life. He did all this for us. He died our death. He was buried instead of us. The conclusion of the Bible is: he was raised for us. The point? His resurrection-his coming out of death-was done for us so that we could come out of death and possess a fresh new life! No gang leader, mom, dad, or friend ever did that for you.

"Therefore we, sharing his death through our baptismal immersion, were with him laid in the grave, in order that, as Christ was raised to life from among the dead, through his Father's glorious power, we, too, might pursue our course in the possession of fresh life." It's a second chance.

The experience of water baptism will help you remember what Jesus did for you. That will help you run to God when you are being tempted to live in the junk that put Jesus on the cross and in the grave to begin with-our sin.

I encourage you to be water baptized as soon as possible. <u>By now, you should belong to a Bible believing church, so ask them!</u>

Think through these issues - especially if they are new thoughts for you. Focus your mind on them until they stick. The devil will fight you over this.

The thoughts I am sharing with you are truths from the Bible. The Bible refers to itself as the "sword of the Spirit." As a soldier, you need to learn to focus on the truths of the Bible to counter-attack the devil when you are feeling pulled away from God (and you will!). As you wield the "sword of the Spirit", you will cause Satan and his dark forces to back off. The Bible says, "Resist the evil, and he will flee from you."

Questions:

1. What attitudes or actions do you need to re-learn?

2. There is a part of you that wants to do right and a part that wants to do wrong. What is your understanding of this WAR going on within you?

3. What is the best way to deal with temptation to do wrong?

4. Explain the "great exchange."

7
The Bible

If you have not already, you need to read my life story. The way that I got saved was absolutely crazy. To put it in a nutshell, I was living in Marinette, Wisconsin and an investigator from social services had taken my three sons from me, Joseph, James, and Marcus, and charged me with child abuse. The charges were absolutely crazy! Oh they got whoopings, but not child abuse.

The local police department was trying to accuse me of being a drug dealer, but at that point, I was using more than I was selling. After they had released me from jail, I had it in my mind that I would kill the social worker. My anger and frustration were at an all time high. I felt hopeless and the death angel had a tight hold on me.

Then, for some strange reason, something spoke to my spirit. Yes me – a heathen! I started praying and reading a Bible a friend had given me.

Now remember, I'm still smoking weed. For four months I read that bible while smoking weed. That was a trip! You know reading all these stories for the first time "under the influence". But all that time, I had no idea there were people praying for me.

Finally, I contacted a homie of mine who had just starting serving God, Willie O. Coates. He was now a pastor. He informed me that I was being drawn to God. I told him that I wanted to come to his church in South Bend, Indiana to be saved. He laughed, telling me, "Boy you can be saved right there where you're at!"

Not long after that, while reading the Bible, I found in the scriptures "When the Son sets you free, you're free indeed." Alone in an empty closet, with my last joint smoked, half-high and desperate, I clumsily called on God and got saved on the spot.

Now let me just say this. The moment I was saved, I no longer smoked weed.

The Bible became real and became a blueprint for my life.

You are going to love God's book, the Bible. As you become familiar with it, the Bible will become a vital part of your spiritual journey. Sitting down with the Bible is like a visit with Jesus. It gives you his thoughts about life and will reveal wonderful secrets about how God wants you to live and relate to him and to others.

"The whole Bible was given to us by inspiration from God and is useful to teach us what is true and to make us realize what is wrong in our lives; it straightens us out and helps us do what is right. It is God's way of making us well prepared at every point, fully equipped to do good to everyone."

The Bible is literally God speaking to you. You can't really get to know God by how you feel. You can't get to know him through experience alone. You can't get to know him by trying to figure him out. The only safe way to get to know God is through what he says about himself in the Bible. This, coupled with journeys in prayer, is the only sure way.

Some General Facts

The Bible is actually a compilation of 66 individual books written by 40 different writers. These people came from varied backgrounds. They were also judges, sheepherders, priests, statesmen, kings, poets, musicians, philosophers, farmers, tax collectors, physicians, tentmakers, and fisherman. The books of the Bible were written over a period of 1600 years. Its chapters were written in palaces and in prisons, in cities and in the wilderness, in times of war and peace, and during a host of other circumstances.

Can you imagine if you had 40 different writers discussing medical science, physics, or any other discipline over a period of 1600 years? There would be much disagreement and a total lack of continuity between writers and time periods.

Yet the Bible, the Word of God, with all its different writers over such a long period of time, is harmonious. It is a divine library filled with history, law, poetry, songs, stories, letters, oratory, parables, drama, philosophy, and sermons.

It has a unity that is self-consistent in explaining God's purpose and dream for the human race. Amazing! The only intelligent answer for this is that One Person authored it through the minds of others.

2 Peter 1:21 says, "No prophecy (or Scripture) ever came from what a man wanted to say. But men led by the Holy Spirit spoke words from God."

2 Timothy 3:16 says, "All Scripture is God-breathed."

The Bible came from God through the people who wrote it. God directed these people so that, through their individual personalities, we get to hear God's message to man.

The Bible is divided into two major sections: the Old Testament and the New Testament. It is conveniently broken down into chapters and verses (not by the original authors). Take a Bible verse like John 3:16. "John" refers to the particular book within the Bible. Each book can be conveniently located in the table of contents at the front of any Bible. The number "3" refers to the chapter within the book. The number following the colon":16" refers to the verse within the chapter.

There are many different versions available at bookstores today. Versions are just various renderings of the same original text that was written in the Hebrew and Greek languages. Look at several different versions (also called translations) in your local

Christian bookstore and decide which one you prefer to read. Make sure you get a bible that you understand, not just a cute one or the same one as your momma. (But thank God for momma.)

History in Advance

Another amazing aspect of the Bible that sets it apart from all other religious books is something called prophecy. Prophecy is a statement of history in advance. God sees the future better than we can remember our past.

There were 333 prophecies in the Bible foretelling the birth, life, death, burial, and resurrection of Jesus Christ. These prophecies were given hundreds of years before Jesus was born and had specific detail in them. Every single one of them came true.

No other book in the entire world has the proven prophetic claims that the Bible has.

The odds for 333 prophecies given in the Old Testament coming to pass in one person's life was 1 out of 870,000,000,000,000,000,000,000,000,000,000, 000,000,000,000,000,000,000,000,000,000,000,000 000,000,000,000,000,000,000!

This same book prophesies the return of Jesus Christ. Jesus said in John 14:1-3, "Do not let you hearts be troubled. Trust in God; trust also in me. In my Father's house are many rooms; if it were not so, I would have told you. I am going there to prepare a place for you. And if I go and prepare a place for you, I will come back and take you to be with me that you may also be where I am."

What if that is true?

Even if we didn't have faith, the historical record demands that we can and should trust God's word, the Bible.

How to Study the Bible

Perhaps you have heard of the endless debates and arguments the so-called "experts" of theology have had over what the Bible really means. If so, you may be wondering how the "common man" could ever understand it. But realize that the issues of debate among "the experts" are over minor technical points, not over the bulk of the biblical text.

It is true that some of the Bible will confuse you at first because you don't understand the historical or theological context in which something is being said (Yes, thankfully, there are many study helps available at Christian bookstores). However, if you stay prayerful and open, most of it will come across very straightforward and simple. You will get it. Don't feel retarded! After all these years I've been saved, I still get confused sometimes. I just give it to God and stand on my faith.

Approach Scripture in the following way:

1. Read and study with an open heart. A few moments in prayer before your study time will help ensure an open heart.

2. Be open to changing the way you think as you read the Bible. Remember, you cannot understand God by what you have experienced or by what you feel. When you see God's point of view on various subjects such as money, family living, ethical choices, etc., decide if you must change if you have believed something else.

3. Expect God to speak to you as you read the Bible. The most common way this happens is through an "Aha" moment – something about the text sticks out to you and you understand how it applies to you or to a situation you are going through. As this understanding comes, ask the Holy Spirit to help you put the truth into practice.

4. Keep the context in mind. There are three types of context in the Bible:

Verse context – Consider the verses which precede and follow the verse you are studying. Many people pull verses right out of their setting to create or support wrong ideas.

Passage context – Always look at a passage in the light of others addressing the same subject. Make sure you have at least two or three verses that say the same thing before you begin to accept a truth.

Covenant context – The Bible is divided into an Old Testament (or covenant) and a New Testament. Since Christianity is based upon the teachings of the New Testament, you are better off familiarizing yourself with the New Testament before trying to tackle an understanding of the Old Testament. Because many Old Testament laws and rules no longer apply to us, be sure to interpret everything taught in the Old Testament in the light of the New Testament.

Always ask yourself four basic questions as you study:
- Who is being spoken to?
- What is being said?
- What does it mean to me?
- How do I apply it practically in my life?

Many Benefits

Choosing to read and study the Bible will release many blessings in your life:

It will cause your life to be fruitful and prosperous (Joshua 1:8; Psalm 1:2-3).

It will uncover sin and error in your thoughts and actions (Hebrews 4:12; Romans 12:2).

It will do an effective work within you (I Thessalonians 2:13).

It will cleanse you (John 15:3; Ephesians 5:25-26).

It will guide you in life (Proverbs 6:21-22; 2 Timothy 3:16-17).

It will keep you from being destroyed when the evil one comes (Isaiah 5:13-14; Hosea 4:6; Matthew 4:4,7,10; Ephesians 6:17; Psalm 105:20).

It is like seed that, after a season, will bring back a harvest of good things (Mark 4:14,20).

It will nourish and build your faith (1 Peter 2:1-2; Romans 10:17).

It will bring you encouragement and help you stick in there when you feel you can't go on (Romans 15:4) It will show you secrets about God that you would have never discovered (1 Corinthians 2:9-10).

A Daily Intake

Jesus said in Matthew 4:4, "It is written: 'Man does not live on bread alone, but on every word that comes from the mouth of God.'"

If you take time to put food into your body daily, take time to put God's bread, the Bible, into your heart daily. Set aside a time to read and think deeply on (meditate) his word.

Without food your body would eventually grow weak and even die. The same holds true for your faith. It is impossible to grow or remain strong in faith without an adequate diet of God's word.

Questions

1. If the Bible is really God speaking to you, how should you approach it?

2. What is the greatest proof of the divine authorship of the Bible?

3. What two benefits from reading and studying the Bible are you most interested in?

4. Read Psalm 119:105. Explain how God's word can be a "lamp" and a "light" to you.

5. What are some of the dangers of a careless reading or studying of God's word?

6. According to Psalm 1:2, we are to "meditate" on God's word "day and night". Why would that be good and what are some practical ways you could start to do that?

8
Praying Soldiers

One of the episodes in which I was shot five times, I ended up in the hospital with three bullet holes in my arm and two in my chest.

The three shots in my arm went straight through, but the two .38 slugs that went into my chest never came out. The x-rays could not find them.

It was years later, after being born again, that a Christian chiropractor found the bullets lodged in front of my heart. I should have died on the spot. I walked around all those years thinking I was "Da Man" and could not be killed. I was that bad... or at least I thought that.

A few months later, I went to visit my grandmother, Nana, in Beloit, Wiconsin. We had communion with God early in the morning, as was her practice for years. In her very quiet, godly voice, she told me how proud she was that I was now saved and serving God.

Then she brought her prayer box out. The first card on the top had my name on it and the date she had started praying for me. Every morning, for 19 and a half years, she prayed that God would protect me and that the blood of Jesus would keep me from all harm. She literally prayed a fence of protection around me.

Talk about a frontline praying soldier!

I think the best part of the journey of faith is having talks with God. We can talk to God and he will respond to us. This dialogue is called prayer.

Think of it. We can actually communicate with the Creator of the universe! He said in Jeremiah 33:3, "Call to me, and I will answer you, and I will tell you great and mighty things, which you do not know." What a promise! There's no call waiting, busy signal, or message center. Now that's what I call a straight up connect!

Don't feel bad if you don't know how to approach God in prayer. When you learn some basics, you will find prayer as easy as breathing or even talking to some of your homies.

God is Spirit

Jesus said in John 4:24, "God is spirit, and his worshipers must worship in spirit and in truth."

Because God has chosen to rule from a spiritual dimension, you cannot contact him through your mind or emotions alone. The way you enter his dimension and establish contact is through focused prayer. Focused prayer is basically directing your essence, the innermost part of your being toward God with an open heart. The Apostle Paul said in Ephesians 6:18, "Pray in the Spirit at all times. Pray with all kinds of prayers, and ask for everything you need." But keep in mind, God is not Santa Clause.

Praying the Scriptures

The greatest way to join your heart for focused prayer is by thinking deeply upon small portions of Scripture as you quiet yourself in a private place. Just as an anchor plunges deep to the ocean floor to secure a ship, the Scriptures will pull your mind deep into the core of your being to secure focused prayer.

Take a verse like Romans 5:8, "But God demonstrates His own love for us in this: while we were still sinners, Christ died for us."

Let your mind settle on the words. Think deeply on what God is saying to you.

This verse suggests that God was committed to us before we ever showed any signs of responding to Him. While we were sinners, Christ gave His all for us!

As you meditate on a verse like this, you will find your mind settling and his presence will begin to be felt deep within you. You have two choices here; either you can continue to read other passages and let him speak to you through them or you can turn from the passage itself and just worship and adore him in his presence. At first you may struggle finding the place of focused prayer. Your mind may fight you with to-do lists and worries, but with practice you will get there. It takes time to learn to pray effectively.

The Kingdom is Within

Remember that effective prayer focuses inside, not outside, of you. Jesus said in Luke 17:21, "people cannot say, 'Look, God's kingdom is here!' or, 'There it is!' No, God's kingdom is within you."

You will make a great mistake if you only look up into the sky to try to enter God's presence. Yes, God is in a real heaven, but he has also made his home in you through the presence of the Holy Spirit.

"Don't you know that you yourselves are God's temple and that God's Spirit lives in you?"

This is not suggesting that you are God, but that God is in you! Your prayer experience is a time to yield and present your heart to the One who is present within you. As you approach him in this inner way, you will be thrilled as he enlightens and leaves "knowings" in you (times when you feel like he is speaking to you – sometimes as words, other times as impressions.)

Remember that your mind can be the greatest enemy to a focused prayer life. Tame it with Scriptures. Take small portions and settle your mind. For some reason, meditation on Scripture will lead you directly to God's secret place deep within you.

This will not always be easy. In fact, at times it may seem exceptionally difficult to enter focused prayer. It will seem like God has left you alone. But that is a lie. Don't buy into that. It is not true. Hebrews 13:5 declares, "God has said, "Never will I leave you; never will I forsake you."

Just determine to use God's Word and in your time with him in prayer, you will discover that prayer will be the key to releasing God's power into your life and into the lives of those you love.

Concerning prayer, the Apostle James said, "The earnest (heartfelt, continued) prayer of a righteous man makes tremendous power available, dynamic in its working."

He is Reaching Out to You!

Another important perspective to maintain in developing a life of prayer is understanding the nature of prayer. If you are not cautious, you will view prayer as man's attempt to contact God. Nothing could be further from the truth!

Jesus proclaims to the church in Revelation 3:20, "Look! I have been standing at the door and I am constantly knocking. If anyone hears me calling him and opens the doors, I will come in and fellowship with him and he with me."

He is calling out to you. He wants you to open your consciousness to him, to call upon him and to seek him. Any thought or desire that comes up within you to seek God is a direct result of his "knocking" or drawing you to himself... not something you came up with on your own. (See John 6:44-45.)

Whenever we follow "the urge" to pray or look into the Scriptures, it may seem like we are reaching out to him, but we are actually responding to him. The Scriptures say in Romans 3:11, "There is no one who understands, no one who seeks God." We would never have thought to pray or to go to his word had he not put that within us to do so. The desire to do these things is the result of his knocking or seeking us!

What a motivator to pray. The God of the universe is seeking you! Make sure you respond and spend time with Him in prayer.

Get More Information

There are so many wonderful benefits to prayer. There are also many specific guidelines for prayer given to us in the Scriptures. Unfortunately, sharing about these wonderful truths is beyond the scope of this writing, but I urge you to go to a local Christian bookstore and ask for some books on prayer.

You will discover that you can change not only your house, school, and hood, but you can change the course of history with effective prayer. Wow! What are you going to do with that?

Questions

1. Why do you think Satan would have us believe that prayer is difficult and needs to be done "just right" to be effective?

2. Explain in your own words the process of using Scripture for focused prayer.

3. How does the Bible say that prayer is a response to God rather than our attempt to initiate contact with him?

4. Find some Bible verses to take with you to settle your mind during times of prayer.

9
Da New Family

Back in the day, we were that notorious family that exists in every hood, down the street from the block. Everybody came to our crib… the drug dealers, the customers, the pimps, the hoes, and anybody else who ran the streets.

It was the one place where everyone was welcomed, but if you were weak, you often became a victim. My momma, PJ as most people called her, would cook for anyone who stopped by. She was friendly to everyone so most of the time, you'd find people catering to her. But when she was upset, momma would lock down the whole house with a nasty attitude.

One day everybody was trippin' on her and she actually set our house on fire! Nope, it wasn't an accident. She sat down in her chair and watched it burn, just waiting for the fire department to show up. The craziest thing was we didn't even have any fire insurance! Like my Nana always said… STUPID! Now tell me, do you think our family needed therapy or what?

As a kid, I thought everyone lived like that: The traffic, the rats, the roaches, the parents screaming, and everyone acting psychotic. You know - total chaos. I was at risk and didn't even know it until years later when I began to act out those same bad habits I had been taught. Violence was all around me and soon that cancer spread to me.

My brothers and I fought all the time. When I was older, my brother Turf and I got into a violent argument over nothing. We fought on and off all day long. I cut off part of his finger. He scolded me with hot water. All of this happened in full view of my mom, dad, my brothers and sisters. I had left the house and went to get my pistol. When I returned, I ran into our bedroom where his girlfriend was weeping, holding his bloody hand. I put a gun in his face and emptied it. The only sane thing that happened was he didn't die.

It was all a way of life for our family. Violence and survival were all we knew, even if it meant feuding with the people closest to us. Hurting people hurt other people and unfortunately, sometimes it's our family.

Thank God for "Da new family".

When I became a Christian, I was surrounded by simple, loving, Christian farmers that were not hung up on religion. I look back now with a laugh and a smile as I remember them bringing me potatoes and corn. Don't laugh. At that point, I didn't have any money and my little bit of faith was out there.

I had heard money cometh, but mine hadn't came yet. I guess God was sending it by mule. Thank God for "Da New Family".

When you decided to become a soldier for Jesus you became a member of the whole family of seekers on the earth – God calls us the 'Church'.

I am not referring to a particular denomination like Lutheran, Catholic, Methodist, etc. People create denominations to organize large groups of people. The actual Church of Jesus Christ cannot be confined to one building or one organization.

You have spiritual brothers, sisters, mothers, and fathers all over the world you haven't met. They attend different churches and denominations but do share one thing in common with you; they have decided to become fully devoted followers of Jesus Christ. They are your new family…da family.

In Matthew 12, starting in verse 47, a man approached Jesus and said, "Your mother and brothers are waiting for you outside. They want to talk to you." Then he (Jesus) pointed to his followers and said, "See! These people are my mother and my brothers. My true brothers and sisters and mother are those who do the things that my Father in heaven wants."

To enjoy the benefit as a member of the family of God (the Church) you must learn how to relate to your new family. You do so in two ways. First, realize you are a part of the global church of Jesus Christ. Everyone who is a follower of Jesus is part of this family.

<u>Secondly, find a local church group with which to get involved.</u>

Here is a checklist to help you track down a good local church.

1. Does the pastor teach practical messages directly from the Bible?

2. Does the church encourage people to ask Jesus to occupy a greater role in their lives?

3. Do they offer more than one service per week for you to grow in your faith?

4. Are they willing to help you personally with your growth in Christ as a disciple?

If you can't find a church that meets all the above criteria, go to the one in which you feel most comfortable. It is very important to establish a relationship as quickly as possible with people who love God like you do.

The Scriptures say, "Bad company corrupts good morals." 1 Corinthians 15:33

Some of you have some bad friends, boyfriends, and girlfriends you need to fire right now!

Often you must get away from old friends and familiar places because they will hinder your growth in faith. A good local church can help you during this critical time. It is when you plant yourself in a local church that you can really begin to take root and grow in your faith. Begin your search immediately!

Questions

1. Why is the Church called your new "family"?

2. Why can't the Church be confined to one building or denomination?

3. Explain why it is important to carefully evaluate a church you are considering joining.

4. Why is it important to be established (regularly attending and involved) in a local church?

10
Wow! They Might Hate Me

I was so excited after I became a born again Christian. Everywhere I went I talked about Jesus. Everything that came out of my mouth was about the gospel. Jesus is Lord. If I said it once, I said it a thousand times.

What really excited me was the opportunity I faced of sharing it with my brothers and sisters. I knew that witnessing to them I had to be extremely cautious as all they knew was the "old", violent man –the man that had attacked them on numerous occasions over the years.

One day, I called my mother's house and was speaking to everyone who was there, doing my witnessing thing when my sister Pat popped up on the phone and sarcastically she said, "Oh you saved now? You changed?"

My first impulse was to reach through the phone and slap the black off her, but that was my flesh talking. "Yes," I said in a calm voice, "And you need to be saved too." Then she screamed, "N*#$@, I've been saved for 25 years!"

I was blown away. How could she make this confession when, at that time, she was a dope addict, a bank robber, and a master thief barred from every grocery store within 50 miles of South Bend, Indiana.

To me, it was a straight up insult, and enough to make me want to rip her head off. It was as though she was mocking my choice to serve God, as though my relationship with Him would be as fake as hers was with no depth. It was then I realized that everyone would not be excited that I had changed. It was almost as though she wished I had remained the same.

It was that experience that forced me to master the art of dealing with rejection for the sake of the gospel.

"If the world hates you, keep in mind that it hated me first." –Jesus

I was upset and sad when I first discovered not everyone shared my enthusiasm for Jesus after I gave my life to Him. I wasn't prepared for the rejection I received and it shook me a little at first. I almost stopped following the God. But I knew being a fully devoted follower of Jesus means we must be willing to follow him no matter who rejects us for it. Thankfully, I ran into something Jesus said to encourage his followers when facing rejections for following him.

Jesus said in John 15:19-20, "The world would love you if you belonged to it; but you don't for I chose you to come out of the world, and so it hates you. Do you remember what I told you? 'A slave isn't greater than his master!' So since they persecuted me, naturally they will persecute you."
Sometimes members of your own family will turn against you. That is really tough. But Jesus warned that we

might face that kind of heartache when choosing to follow him:

"Don't imagine that I came to bring peace to the earth! No, rather, a sword. I have come to set a man against his father, and a daughter against her mother, and a daughter-in-law against her mother-in-law... a man's worst enemies will be right in his own home! If you love your father and mother more than you love me, you are not worthy of being mine; or if you love your son or daughter more than you love me, you are not worthy of being mine. If you refuse to take up your cross and follow me, you are not worthy of being mine. If you cling to your life, you will lose it; but if you give it up for me, you will save it."

These verses are a little hard to understand, but Jesus is simply saying that when you follow him, it will sometimes create problems between you and people you love. However, we must still choose to love him more than any human being on earth.

What Makes Them Mad?

The first murder in history happened between two brothers, Cain and Abel. The Bible tells us that it occurred because Cain felt guilty and ashamed of his actions when he saw the right actions of his brother Abel. Hatred arose in Cain because Abel's good deeds made the evil deeds of Cain even more evil looking. There is something in all of us that wants to cover up and not face the wrong we do.

"Do not be like Cain, who belonged to the evil one and murdered his brother. And why did he murder him? Because his own actions were evil and his brother's were righteous? Do not be surprised brothers, if the world hates you."

Because of your alliance with Jesus, there is a purity and a wholesomeness about you. That purity and wholesomeness intimidates others who are not followers of the Lord. It is this intimidation that will often cause the people you love to respond defensively and negatively toward you. That is why John says in the verse quoted above, "Don't be surprised, my brothers, if the world hates you."

I am not suggesting that everyone will hate you. Many people will love you and accept you when you share your new life with them. The point is your allegiance with Jesus will bring strong reactions either way… you need to decide ahead of time to just focus on loving Jesus no matter who it separates you from or associates you with.

When someone does reject you because of your new faith in Jesus, don't retaliate and get mad at them. These people are not rejecting you. They are really rejecting Jesus. Just love them and pray for them. God will work through your prayers and through the love that you show them. In time, they will come to the place where they will be more open to faith and may respond and decide to become followers of Christ.

Meanwhile, Jesus promises new relationships to those who are forced to retreat from family and friends because of their new found faith by saying, "I tell you the truth. Everyone who has left his home, brothers, sisters, mother, father, children, or fields for me and for the Good News will get a hundred times more than he left. Here in this world he will have more homes, brothers, sisters, mothers, children and fields. And with those things, he will suffer for his belief. But in the age that is coming he will have life forever."

It takes great trust in God to obey him even when family and friends reject you for it! But it you do it, you will find that he will fulfill this promise. He will bring you many times more friends (other followers of Jesus) who will love and support you than those who have rejected you for your faith.

Jesus has followers everywhere, in every denomination. If you obey him, he will lead you to them! On top of that, over the years, you will experience the joy of watching the ones who initially rejected you come one by one into the kingdom of God!

Questions

1. Hopefully, many of your family and friends will rejoice when they hear the news of your faith. Unfortunately, some may not. Are you prepared for reactions of family and friends?

2. Think about what it cost Jesus Christ to bring you into relationship with God. When you consider what it cost Jesus to reach you, why does possible rejection by others, even loved ones, not seem so terrible? Is it you they are rejecting? How will you respond to those who reject you?

3. According to Jesus, what are the rewards of handling rejection in a proper manner?

11
Holy Spirit & Fire

I am absolutely amazed by the power of the Holy Spirit. Once I was saved, it became very hard to lie, cheat, or steal. Numerous times I've been in stores and a clerk mistakenly gave me back too much change. I immediately returned it and watched the shock on their faces as I proclaimed, "You know real Christians wouldn't cheat like that, don't you?"

The Holy Spirit is now my teacher, and every day tries to keep me clean and on track. I've always taught in the churches that the same Holy Spirit that draws people into the kingdom of God is the same Holy Spirit that will make new converts pull up their britches and clean up their acts.

Your decision to follow Jesus did not happen on your own. Jesus said, "No one can come to me unless the Father who sent me draws him." But how does God the Father "draw" us to Jesus? He does so by the Holy Spirit.

But who is the Holy Spirit?

He is God.

You might be thinking, "Wait a minute…Jesus is God, the Father is God, and there is the Holy Spirit who is also God?"

At first, this does seem a bit confusing.

But consider that, though God is our Creator and we are made like him, he is also different from us. He is eternal (having no beginning or end), everywhere present, all-knowing and multi-personed. He is a trinity (or three in one). It is hard for us to grasp what makes God, God. There is mystery in the mix. Trying to clearly explain the mystery would be like trying to explain to your dog how humans and dogs differ. He just won't get it. Neither do we.

The closest we can get (and it really isn't that close) is, just like you have different sides to your personality – you have an emotional self, a civic self, a reasoning self, etc., God has different sides to his nature. He is a Father, a Son, and a Holy Spirit. Three very distinct entities, yet he is one.

His different "selves" represent various aspects of his ministry to us as his creation. The Father is the mastermind of creation and author of the will of God. The Son, Jesus, is our Savior and carries out the will of the Father. The Holy Spirit brings enabling power for the Father's will to be done.

You have come to Jesus, the Savior. It is your alliance with him that has brought you "out of darkness into his marvelous light." As you grow in your faith and in your knowledge of God's word, you will discover that Jesus' ministry will help you overcome temptation (Hebrews 2:18; 4:15-16; 12:2). And if you ignore his help there, he will come to your aid whenever you fail and sin (I John 2:1-2).

As you continue pursuing spiritual growth through Bible study and prayer, you will learn more of the Fatherhood of God and you will watch his destiny unfold in your life.

In this chapter, we'll focus on the role of the Holy Spirit in our lives.

The Person of the Holy Spirit

When Jesus was getting ready to physically leave this planet, he made a striking statement about the Holy Spirit. He said in John 16:7, "But I tell you the truth: It is for your good that I am going away. Unless I go away, the Counselor (Holy Spirit) will not come to you; but if I go, I will send him to you."

He was saying that his disciples would be better off if he were not physically on this planet. That had to be sort of hard to believe. As long as Jesus was around, he taught them how to pray (Luke 11:1). He explained the Bible to them (Luke 24:32). He gave them direction for their lives (Matthew 10:5). He showed them the power of God (Matthew 8:26-27).

How could it be to their advantage for him to leave?

The answer is in what he offered them in return. He said when he left he would send "the Comforter", or the Holy Spirit. Now he, the Holy Spirit, would teach us how to pray; "But you, dear friends, build yourselves up in your most holy faith and pray in the Holy Spirit." (Also see Romans 8:26)

Now the Holy Spirit explains the Bible to us: "But when He, the Spirit of truth, comes, He will guide you into all truth."

Now he gives us direction for our lives: "Because those who are led by the Spirit of God are sons of God."

Now he brings us the power of God: "But you will receive power when the Holy Spirit comes on you."

Everything Jesus was to the disciples, the Holy Spirit would be that, and more! To connect with Jesus in those days you had to wait in line. You also had to find where the line was! He was pretty elusive (Mark 1:36-37). But Jesus promised that the Holy Spirit would be as close as a prayer from an open heart. No hunting him down. No standing in line. The Holy Spirit is God's always-and everywhere-present connection to the believer.

Getting To Know the Holy Spirit

2 Corinthians 13:14 says, "May the grace of the Lord Jesus Christ, and the love of God, and the fellowship of the Holy Spirit be with you all."

The word "fellowship" used here means deep communion and intimacy.

Just as you were introduced to the ministry of Jesus, you must be introduced to the ministry of the Holy Spirit.

Actually the Holy Spirit came into your heart the moment Jesus did – you can't divide God. However, the Holy Spirit does not call attention to himself. He points us to the ministry of Jesus and the Father. John 16:13 says of the Holy Spirit, "He will not speak on his own; he will speak only what he hears, and he will tell you what is yet to come."

He is like the silent guest of a friend you have invited into your home. You first focus on your friend for a moment or two and then you look over to see whom he brought. Your friend then introduces you to this new person.

Jesus is the one who introduces the believer to the Holy Spirit. The Bible calls this introduction being "baptized" with the Holy Spirit. John the Baptist said concerning Jesus in Matthew 3:11, "I baptize you with water for repentance. But after me will come one who is more powerful than I, whose sandals I am not fit to carry. He will baptize you with the Holy Spirit and with fire."

Being baptized into something or someone means you are immersed into them. Have you ever met a person whose impression stayed with you – you seem to have been immersed into their personality? In the baptism of the Holy Spirit you are introduced to the person and ministry of the Holy Spirit. His character and essence will make an overwhelming impression on you.

Jesus described these experiences in the Gospel of john. In one place, while explaining what happens to a person who initially opens their heart to faith, he compared the experience with drinking in water: "but whoever drinks of the water that I shall give him shall never thirst; but the water that I shall give him shall become in him a well of water springing up to eternal life."

Everyone who has received Christ can testify to the sense of being filled within.

Later in John 7:37-38 it says, "Now on the last day, the great day of the feast, Jesus stood and cried out saying, 'If any man is thirsty, let him come to me and drink. He who believes in me, as the Scripture has said, 'From his innermost being shall flow rivers of living water.'"

Note that this is a description of more than a simple "drinking in" of living water – it is a description of an experience that leads to an explosive "river" that bursts from within. That is what receiving the Holy Spirit is like. (We know that Jesus is referring to the Holy Spirit when he refers to "rivers" flowing out of us because the next verse says, "By this he meant the Spirit, whom those who believed in him were later to receive.")

Receiving the Baptism of the Holy Spirit

To experience Holy Spirit baptism you should follow these simple guidelines:

Guideline 1 - Realize that in this experience you are not receiving a different Holy Spirit. There is only one Holy Spirit and he came into your life when you opened your heart to Jesus.

Romans 8:9 tells us that anyone who receives Jesus Christ already has the Holy Spirit in his life: "And if anyone does not have the Spirit of Christ, he does not belong to Christ."

Sincere followers of Jesus already have the Holy Spirit present in their hearts. He is the reason believers feel peace or joy in their faith. Galatians 5:22 says that, "the fruit of the Spirit is love, joy, peace, patience, kindness, goodness, faithfulness, gentleness, and self-control." Being baptized into the Holy Spirit just means you are going to be immersed into these wonderful traits a little more powerfully.

There is no need for anxiety here. You will meet firsthand the same, familiar, warm and precious Holy Spirit who drew you to Christ in the first place.

Guideline 2 - Open your heart to receive the Holy Spirit. The Holy Spirit comes as a gift from God. Luke 11:13 says, "If you then, though you are evil, know how to give good gifts to your children, how much more will your

Father in heaven give the Holy Spirit to those who ask him!"

Just as with any gift, the Holy Spirit must be received. When the Apostle Paul met some believers in Acts 19:2, he asked them, "Did you receive the Holy Spirit when you believed?"

Why did he ask that? Wasn't the Holy Spirit already in their lives? Absolutely. But having the Holy Spirit doesn't mean you have received the ministry of the Holy Spirit.

Guideline 3 - When you come to God to receive the Holy Spirit, you must come to him with a totally open and yielded heart.

To help you get to that point, I would highly recommend that you spend a good portion of time worshipping God and telling him how much you love him. Then when you have prayed as far into his presence as you can and you sense his presence dawning on you, say to the Lord, "Father, I receive the Holy Spirit in Jesus' Name."

The Holy Spirit's Leading

"Those who are led by the Spirit of God are sons of God."

According to Scripture, the Holy Spirit is the One who leads us into truth and the One who gives us direction for our lives. As followers of God, it is important for us to discover his methodology.

Often, the Holy Spirit leads us or speaks to us in ways that are very subtle. Catching his lead can be tricky because he is so gentle. Often we can miss what he is trying to communicate to us because of our busyness and because of the level of ambient noise in our lives.

Here are some simple guidelines to follow to uncover the leading of the Holy Spirit:

1. Does the direction you feel the Holy Spirit is giving you contradict the Bible? If so, it cannot be the leading of God! He would never tell you to go rob a bank, because the bible clearly tells us to obey the laws of the land.

2. Would the direction you feel the Holy Spirit is giving you cause harm to yourself or someone else? If so, it cannot be from God. He loves people and only wants good to come into our lives. For instance, God would never tell you to divorce your spouse and go marry your next-door neighbor! God's will is to repair and heal, not discard.

3. Ask people who have been followers of Jesus for a while (perhaps a pastor or committed Christian friend) what he or she thinks about it. Often, by getting help from someone who knows God, we can get solid counsel that brings us clarity.

4. Is the direction that you feel is from God causing a lot of confusion in your mind? If so, it might be a sign that something isn't right! Keep in mind that part of the Holy Spirit's "job" on earth is to be of help to us. He is not our servant, but He is the liaison between heaven and earth. One of the meanings of the word used in the original language of the New Testament for the Holy Spirit is "the One called along side to help."

He is here to comfort, lead, guide, teach, and reveal to us all God has for us in this life!

Questions

1. Did it ever occur to you before being born-again that you could know God, be in His family, rely on Him for help? You don't have to stand in line to get Jesus to help you or hear you. According to I Corinthians 6:19, how close is He?

2. The Holy Spirit actually drew you to Jesus. Recall the events leading up to accepting Christ. Does it seem now that the Holy Spirit was moving in your life, getting you prepared for receiving Christ?

3. What is the Holy Spirit commissioned to do on your behalf here on earth?

12
Prisoner Of The American Dream

You have an inheritance…and it's not the "American dream".

Right after I was saved, I wrote a book about my life story called, "Prisoner of the American Dream." It isn't a cute title, but it actually meant something.

From the moment we're put here on the earth, we're taught that to be successful, you have to achieve the American dream: The house on the hill, the white picket fence, the two car garage, 2.5 children, the car, the credit cards, money in the bank, etc.

That's an outright lie. It's not about all that. It's about finding purpose and fulfilling your destiny. It's about your relationship with God.

I believe that God actually allowed me to experience the so-called American dream while I was living in San Diego, California. I had the big homes, swimming pools, jewelry, and all the other stuff. I was always hustling, trying to get more. The more I got, the more I wanted.

I once paid cash for a Rolls Royce after a white salesman in Point Loma had snubbed me earlier in the day. He mistook me for nothing but a poor, little, black slave boy from the plantation with no chance of ever owning a Rolls Royce.

Get serious! When I returned that evening with a paper bag full of cash, everything changed. Now I was "da man". It was all about the bank. Legal or illegal money, it made no difference to him. Now I had the power and the salesman was reduced to the idiot he was.

I lived for today, enjoying the American dream bit by bit. Sometimes I would pull to the side of the road and pick up hitch hikers in my Rolls just to blow their minds. I was high and laughed all the time. It was my lifeline.

One day, Byron Payne, one of my lieutenants and I, were driving up and down the coast of California. We came upon the "Western White House" where President Richard Nixon lived in San Clemente. We thought it would be cool to stop by and check it out. When we turned onto the property, we immediately saw the secret service. As we came up to the security gate totally stoned, we laughed and told them we wanted to see the president.

Now you can imagine, all they could probably think about was putting these two crazy negroes in jail. By the grace of God, they simply told us to leave the property immediately or we would be arrested. Wow! What a trip!

Kids don't do drugs.

Seriously, life is not about a new car, money, the American dream, or even meeting the president. There will always be somebody who has bigger and better. Solomon says in the book of Ecclesiastes, "It's all a blowing in the wind. It doesn't mean anything. The only thing that matters is our relationship with God."

But let me tell you about our inheritance we have with God.

What if you were informed of the death of a distant relative who made provision for you in his will, making you an heir to his fortune? Wouldn't that be great?

Well, when Jesus ascended to Heaven, he made special provision for us. The Bible says in Romans 8:17, "Now if we are children, then we are heirs – heirs of God and co-heirs with Christ."

In Ephesians 1:18 Paul the apostle said, "I pray also that the eyes of your heart may be enlightened in order that you may know the riches of his glorious inheritance." Because of this inheritance, life can be easier for us.

God wants us to discover his inheritance so that our lives can be enriched. He doesn't want us to wander around in life wondering where we will end up. As children of God, we have an inheritance, we can change the direction of our lives on purpose! In a sense, we can choose our future.

God said, "I call heaven and earth to witness against you today, that I have set before you life and death, the blessing and the curse. So choose life in order that you may live."

How much joy you have, how successful you are in a career or as a student, how good your marriage or singleness is, how much money you have, how healthy you are, can all be pre-determined by whether or not you cooperate with God and his inheritance for you.

You don't have to wait, wonder or wander to find out where your life is headed. You don't have to be a victim of society or circumstances. Your past experiences don't have to dominate you any longer!

Jesus said in Mark 9:23, "Everything is possible for him who believes." When you believe in God, you have no boundaries. There is nothing too big for him. It may take some time for you to learn how to follow him out of your messed up life and into his inheritance for you, but there is never a case where God will say, "You're too messed up... I can't help you!"

Because of his willingness to help us, we become winners! In fact, followers of Jesus are called "more than a conqueror" in Scripture. Isn't that good news?!

There are three essential things you must do to experience God's inheritance.

1. Discover the various aspects of God's inheritance through reading the Scriptures. (Find a good church that can help you locate them!) II Peter 1:3-4 declares, "His divine power has given us everything we need for life and godliness though our knowledge of Him who called us by His own glory and goodness. Through these he has given us his very great and precious promises, so that through them you may participate in the divine nature."

2. Take the promises that you find to God in prayer and ask him to fulfill them for you. He wants to, but he wants us to ask. He won't move in our lives unless we choose to cooperate with him. He's a gentleman. I John 5:14-15 says, "This is the assurance we have in approaching God: that if we ask anything according to his will (the Bible), he hears us. And if we know that he hears us, whatever we ask, we know that we have what we asked of him."

3. After you pray, believe that he has granted what you asked and give him thanks before you see any of the physical evidence of the answered prayer. In Mark 11:24 Jesus said, "Therefore I tell you, whatever you ask in prayer, believe that you have received it and it will be yours."

When Jesus taught his followers about how the kingdom of God operates in our lives, he said, "The kingdom of God is like a man who plants seed in the ground. The seed comes up and grows night and day. It doesn't matter whether the man is asleep or awake; the seed still grows. The man does not know how it grows. Without any help, the earth produces grain. First the plant grows, then the head, and then all the grain in the head. When the grain is ready, the man cuts it. This is harvest time."

Though God will do a quick work at times, he generally moves in a way that is best reflected in the growth cycle of a crop. Harvest, or the end result, doesn't come overnight. It is during this "waiting for the growth " time that we must learn to walk by faith. Walking by faith means you quit judging what is happening by what you see. God will usually work undercover for some time before you see any outward changes. Have a little patience!

God is spirit and he works from the unseen world to the seen world. Just because you don't see any immediate changes, don't get discouraged. God is working! When we trust him, he is always faithful to bring his promised inheritance to pass in your life.

Questions

1. You've heard of a person planning ahead for the time of his death by preparing a "last will and testament." The Bible consists of the Old Testament and the New Testament. That New Testament, or will, has provisions in it for you as a child of God. Just as a will from wealthy family members could enrich your life, how do you suppose being an heir of God could bless your life?

2. If no one contacted you to say you were named in someone's will, you would never receive the inheritance. How do you go about receiving all God has for you?

3. Name three essential steps to experiencing God's inheritance.

13
Remember Your Assignment

Dear friends and brother/sister in Christ,
You have now been given all the necessary information on being what God called you to be in the kingdom of God: A righteous soldier, the ultimate calling on anybody's life.

Just in case you've never accepted Jesus as your Lord and Savior, I want to give you the opportunity to do that right now. Romans 10:9 says, "If you confess with your mouth and believe in your heart that Jesus died for your sins and was resurrected from the dead, you will be saved." All you need to do is say the following prayer.

"Jesus, forgive me for my sins and all the things I've done wrong. I invite you to come into my heart and set me free. I accept you as my Lord and Savior."

It's that simple. Your name has now been written in the book of life.

I pray that you will read your bible, fellowship with God, join a church, and receive your assignment.

We need on fire Christians to join us on the front line of ministry and fill the vacancy of wounded, hurt Christians in the church. The season that is upon us now is a season of spiritual warfare. It's time to put in serious work. Get on it!

If you ever need prayer, or a covering, don't hesitate to call us at the ministry.

In Him we win.

Your brother in Christ,

Joseph

14
"Bad Boy Turned Good" Pictures

"Your past does not dictate your future!"
Lakes Wales, Florida

Joseph sharing his "Choices" message with students
Grand Rapids, Michigan

Signing autographs in St. Maarten

Joseph shares his life story with former President Bush

Coming Fall 2012 to a School Near You!
Dr. Joseph Jennings
"Bullied 2 Bully: *Break the Chain*" Tour

Bad Boy about to turn good!

Paid cash for a Rolls Royce San Diego, California

Layin' money traps Point Loma, California

Playin' in Hollywood with the Funk-A-Delics

About Dr. Joseph Jennings

Former gang leader, Dr. Joseph Jennings, is the President and Founder of Second Chances Outreach Inc., working to carry out the mission of preventing youth violence by providing positive alternatives to gang involvement, bullying, and other high-risk behaviors.

He has written three books including "Prisoner of the American Dream", "Black Man White Man: The Tale of Two Friends", and "Bad Boy Turned Good: A Second Chance" and is currently working on a fourth entitled, "Bullied 2 Bully". Dr. Jennings has appeared on multiple syndicated television and radio programs from Jenny Jones and the Ricki Lake Show to C-SPAN and CBN.

The majority of Dr. Jennings' outreach takes place in the public school systems. From the riot-torn schools of Los Angeles, to the middle class suburbs of Denver; from the toughest schools in Washington, D.C. to the well-heeled neighborhoods of central Florida, Dr. Jennings message is universally embraced.

More than two million young people have benefitted from his powerful and challenging presentations on gangs, violence, bullying, drugs, abstinence, and broken families. His message is not another "scared straight" program, but it's reality.

Dr. Jennings gets results with young people because he can relate. He's been there. Jennings grew up in the ghetto of South Bend, Indiana, the oldest of twelve siblings. He spent years as a gang leader and drug dealer being burned, stabbed, and shot thirteen times.

Dr. Jennings is a true example of a bad boy turned good and proof that our God is truly a God of second chances.

For more information on booking Dr. Joseph Jennings, please contact our office by phone at 770-599-1629 or email at contact@josephjennings.com.